The RAILWAY Magazine
Archive Collection
The 1930s

GRESLEY BOOKS

Introduction — The 1930s

Welcome to this book of railway photographs from the Mortons *Railway Magazine* Archive, concentrating on the very eventful decade of the 1930s. First published in London in 1897, *The Railway Magazine* is one of the oldest titles in the United Kingdom, and I was proud to be its ninth editor from 1989 until 1994. It is now produced by the Mortons Media Group of Horncastle, Lincolnshire, and remains Britain's best-selling railway title.

The 1930s were the golden age of the 'Big Four' railway companies that arose from the Railway Act of 1921 following the experience of placing the country's many diverse railway companies under government control during the First World War. By the time the London, Midland & Scottish Railway, London & North Eastern Railway, Great Western Railway and Southern Railway were born on January 1, 1923, the total UK rail network had grown to a staggering route mileage of almost 19,600.

Among the constituent companies forming the LMS were the London & North Western Railway (which exactly a year earlier had amalgamated with the Lancashire & Yorkshire Railway), the Midland Railway, the Caledonian Railway, the Glasgow & South Western Railway, the Highland Railway, the Furness Railway and the North Staffordshire Railway, not to mention Ireland's Northern Counties Committee. The new company found itself with more than 7000 route miles and well over 10,000 steam locomotives from 393 classes, many of them dating back to the last decades of the 19th century, so a serious programme of standard class locomotive-building was sorely needed.

This did not happen, though, until the appointment of William Stanier from the Great Western Railway as Chief Mechanical Engineer in 1932, for he was preceded in the post by George Hughes from the Lancashire & Yorkshire Railway (1923-25), Sir Henry Fowler from the Midland Railway (1925-31) and Sir Ernest Lemon (1931-32).

Fowler did, however, introduce some much-needed new motive power to the LMS, including the parallel-boiler, three-cylinder express passenger 'Royal Scot' 4-6-0s that were introduced in 1927, and the smaller 'Baby Scot' (or 'Patriot') 4-6-0s in 1930.

Stanier and his drawing office team wasted no time in transforming the face of the LMS by introducing thousands of modern, capable locomotives. The programme began in 1933 with his two-cylinder, taper-boiler 2-6-0s (the first of which even sported a GWR-style top feed cover!) and 'Princess Royal' Pacifics. Other notable new classes were the three-cylinder 'Jubilee' 4-6-0s of 1934 and the mighty 'Princess Coronation' Pacifics of 1937.

Perhaps the two most important designs of all, though, were the versatile mixed-traffic 'Black Five' 4-6-0s, built between 1934 and 1951 and eventually numbering 842 examples, and the freight equivalent, the 8F 2-8-0s of 1935. Although only 126 8Fs had been built by the outbreak of war in 1939, the numbers were massively boosted when the design was adopted as a national standard engine for war service until eventually succeeded by the cheaper WD 2-8-0 'Austerities' (and a number of similarly-styled 2-10-0s) in 1943.

Among the main constituent companies forming the LNER were the Great Northern Railway, the North Eastern Railway, the Great Eastern Railway, the Great Central Railway, the Hull & Barnsley Railway, the North British Railway and the Great North of Scotland Railway, but unlike the LMS, the appointment of Nigel Gresley as the LNER's Chief Mechanical Engineer from his similar post at the Great Northern Railway brought a vital continuation that would earn the newly-founded company a richly-deserved reputation for glamour and speed.

Gresley's hand was seen in many sleek and efficient express locomotive designs, including the A3 Pacifics, the V2 2-6-2s, the mighty P2 2-8-2s and of course his crowning glory, the streamlined A4 Pacifics that launched the superb art deco-styled King's Cross to Newcastle 'Silver Jubilee' express of 1935 (in a trial run for which No. 2509 *Silver Link* attained a record-breaking speed of 112mph).

In 1937, the King's Cross to Edinburgh 'Coronation' brought yet more excitement, and to top it all, in a challenge to a briefly-held German steam speed record of 125mph, A4 Pacific *Mallard* attained the still-standing world record for steam of 126mph on July 3, 1938.

At the Grouping, the LNER's rail network stretched to 6590 miles, and even though some two-thirds of its income came from freight, its main image to this day remains one of glamour.

In comparison to these two giants, the remaining members of the 'Big Four', the Great Western Railway and the Southern Railway inherited route mileages of just 3800 and 2186 respectively.

The GWR, whose identity remained largely unchanged, absorbed a large number of relatively small concerns including Cambrian Railways (along with the narrow-gauge Vale of Rheidol and Welshpool & Llanfair lines), the Alexandra (Newport & South Wales) Docks & Railway, the Barry Railway, the

Brecon & Merthyr Railway, the Burry Port & Gwendraeth Valley Railway, the Cardiff Railway, the Rhymney Railway and the Taff Vale Railway.
From the birth of the 'Big Four' and right through until 1941, the Great Western Railway's Chief Mechanical Engineer was Charles B Collett, who had succeeded the great George Jackson Churchward. Collett and his team successfully introduced many fast, modern locomotives including the four-cylinder 'Castle' and 'King' 4-6-0s, the two-cylinder 'Hall' and 'Grange' 4-6-0s, the delightful 1400 Class 0-4-2 tank engines for branch-line work and a number of versatile prairie and pannier tank classes.
Even Gresley learned valuable lessons following the sure-footed trial running of a 'Castle' out of King's Cross in the 1920s, and at the Grouping, the Great Western Railway was the most standardised company of the 'Big Four', to all intents and purposes carrying on as if nothing much had really happened – and this unique identity continued even into British Railways days.
The Southern Railway differed from the others in that its main business was passenger rather than freight traffic, but at the Grouping, despite its massive commitment to electrification, it found itself with a diverse range of steam locomotives and rolling stock from the companies it had absorbed, including the London & South Western Railway, the London, Brighton & South Coast Railway, the South Eastern Railway and the South Eastern & Chatham Railway, which had been formed in 1899 as a working union between the South Eastern Railway and the London Chatham & Dover Railway.
The SR's first of only two Chief Mechanical Engineers was the Dublin-born Richard Edward Lloyd Maunsell, who retained the post he'd held at the South Eastern & Chatham Railway, and Oliver Bulleid from the LNER who succeeded him in 1937. Among Maunsell's outstanding contributions to the newly-formed company were the four-cylinder 'Lord

YORK After the death of Sir Nigel Gresley following a short illness in 1941, his successor as Chief Mechanical Engineer of the LNER, Edward Thompson, chose the historic *Great Northern* to rebuild as an A1/1 Pacific in 1945, in the process ruining its good looks forever. It was pictured beneath the coaling tower at York MPD.

Nelson' 4-6-0s that uniquely produced eight exhaust beats to the bar and found plenty of work on heavy boat trains. Many 'King Arthur' 4-6-0s were also built during Maunsell's watch, and his three-cylinder V-class 'Schools' 4-4-0s became the most powerful of their type in Britain. The U and U1 2-6-0s, Z class 0-8-0 shunters and W class 2-6-4 tank locomotives were also designed and built under Maunsell, whose name, incidentally, should be pronounced 'Mansell'.

As many photographs in this book show, the 1930s was a decade of bold experimentation in the search for more efficient steam motive power, and the introduction of modern standard locomotives, the benefits of which had already been amply demonstrated by the GWR.

Among the memorable designs were Gresley's 4-6-4 four-cylinder compound No. 10000, featuring a modified Yarrow-built marine-type water-tube boiler working at an ultra-high pressure of 450lb, which emerged from Darlington Works in 1929, and Stanier's steam-turbine 'Turbomotive' No. 6202, the third of his 'Princess Royal' class, which featured a long forward turbine on one side and a short reversing turbine on the other.

Introduced in 1934 to handle the heaviest passenger trains without the need for double-heading on the difficult line between Edinburgh and Aberdeen, another of Gresley's masterpieces was the three-cylinder P2. Six of these gigantic 2-8-2 locomotives were built, featuring 6ft 2in driving wheels and massive boilers, but only nine years later they were rebuilt by Gresley's successor Edward Thompson as not very attractive-looking A2/2 Pacifics.

The sleek A4 Pacifics of the LNER and 'Princess Coronation' Pacifics of the LMS were the outstanding symbols of an all-too-brief 'streamlined age' that was cut short by war in 1939, but even though the GWR 'Castles' could show a clean pair of heels to most locomotives without the need for any tinwork, one of the most bizarre attempts at streamlining appeared on No. 5005 *Manorbier Castle* in 1935. This consisted of a bulbous smokebox door cover, shrouds around the outside cylinders and buffer beam and fairings behind the chimney and safety-valve bonnet, and from the bottom of the cab front right along the running plate.

While it's all too easy to become carried away by the exciting locomotive developments of the 1930s, many of our photographs show that throughout this period, countless pre-grouping locomotives of every

EUSTON A prestigious duty for grimy ex-London & North Western Railway 'Cauliflower' 0-6-0 No. 8442 as it backs the first of William Stanier's streamlined four-cylinder 'Princess Coronation' Pacifics, No. 6220 *Coronation*, into Euston station in 1937, when the Euston to Glasgow 'Coronation Scot' was launched.

The Railway Magazine Archive Collection – The 1930s

kind, many dating from the 19th century, continued to battle on gamely with passenger and goods trains alike.

Many pre-grouping classes toiled away on coal trains for the rest of their days, while large-wheeled 4-4-0s and Atlantics continued their high-stepping ways on express trains, increasingly so as pilot engines. Throughout the 1930, locomotives such as the Great Western 'Bulldog 4-4-0s', London & North Western Railway 'Claughton' 4-6-0s, South Eastern & Chatham Railway Wainwright D 4-4-0s, Highland Railway 'Castle' 4-6-0s, Great Northern Railway Atlantics (4-4-2s) and locomotives of a similar wheel arrangements from the London, Brighton & South Coast, Great Northern, Great Eastern, Great Central and North British Railways could still be seen at work on passenger duties, while a plethora of venerable smaller engines continued to work on branch lines, in shunting yards and as station pilots. Goods and mineral traffic remained the bread and butter of the three biggest 'Big Four' constituents throughout their existence, and while the quest for express train publicity stole the 1930s headlines, it was in vast goods yards and shunting sidings that the real work went on day and night.

If you were a town or city dweller, it's almost certain that you would have heard short whistle blasts carried on the wind and the continuous 'clink, clank' of loose-coupled wagons clashing together as you went upstairs to bed – noises that can still be heard, rather hauntingly, in many old black and white films. After many enjoyable hours of pondering over the Mortons *Railway Magazine* photographic archive, (now, thankfully, digitised) our archivist Jane Skayman and I have endeavoured to present a fair balance from the 1930s, and hope very much that you will enjoy looking at these nostalgic images as much as we have done.

Peter Kelly

GRETNA William Stanier's streamlined Pacifics were preceded by the 'Princess Royals' that were introduced in 1933. In November 1935, over the difficult West Coast Main Line, the second of these, No. 6201 *Princess Elizabeth*, took the world record for the longest and fastest non-stop run for steam traction by averaging 70.1mph over the whole 401 miles between Glasgow Central and London Euston. That same locomotive is seen heading the long and heavy up 'Royal Scot' near Gretna in 1934.

Right: Were these the smallest smoke-deflectors ever devised? The photo, taken in the 1930s, shows the Southern Railway's Eastleigh-built N15 'King Arthur' 4-6-0 No 450 *Sir Kay* fitted with the experimental 'wings'. The locomotive remained in service until 1960.

Below right In the search for more power and efficiency, the 1930s proved to be a decade of diverse experimentation with steam locomotives. In 1929, a joint venture between LMS Chief Mechanical Engineer Sir Henry Fowler and The Superheater Company resulted in the ultra-high-pressure compound 4-6-0 No. 6399 *Fury* being built by the North British Locomotive Company in Glasgow. It featured a high-pressure cylinder between the frames and two lower-pressure outside cylinders, but in February 1930 disaster struck when one of the ultra-high-pressure tubes burst, the steam escaping with such violence that it blasted the coal fire straight through the firehole door. Tragically, this resulted in the death of Lewis Schofield from The Superheater Company, who was on the footplate the time. The boiler was repaired, and trials continued until 1934, but finally the locomotive was rebuilt as a conventional three-cylinder 4-6-0.

Left: **CREWE** Three years after William Stanier moved from the Great Western Railway to become Chief Mechanical Engineer of the LMS in 1932, *Fury* was rebuilt as a conventional three-cylinder 4-6-0, and fitted with an efficient Type 2 Stanier taper boiler. Renamed and renumbered as 'Royal Scot' No. 6170 *British Legion*, it was pictured at Crewe immediately after the transformation in 1935.

Right: **KETTERING** In 1923 the newly-formed London, Midland & Scottish Railway found itself with well over 10,000 steam locomotives from more than 390 classes – and as it began to build large numbers of standard locomotives during the 1930s many of the numbers originally applied to old pre-grouping locos were changed to accommodate new-builds by simply adding 2000. In this evocative scene, former Midland Railway 3F 0-6-0 No. 3042 and 1400 class 2-4-0 No 20216 (formerly No. 216) stand together at Kettering MPD.

Below: **DONCASTER** What a stirring image of times gone by as former Great Northern Railway Ivatt Atlantic No. 3254 pilots former Great Central Railway B2 4-6-0 No. 5424 *City of Lincoln* with a York to Harwich train at Doncaster in July 1939. Note the short articulated carriages in the background. *RMA0793*

Above: **EAST COAST MAIN LINE** Imagine the busy chatter from the chimney of A4 Pacific No. 2509 *Silver Link* as it heads the southbound 'Silver Jubilee' express along the East Coast Main Line in 1938. *Silver Link*, the first of the four light and charcoal grey A4s assigned to the duty (the others being Nos. 2510 *Quicksilver*, 2511 *Silver King* and 2512 *Silver Fox*) attained a record-breaking speed of 112mph during a trial run of the streamlined Kings Cross to Newcastle express that was inaugurated on September 30, 1935. *RMA0842*

BLETCHLEY The 1930s brought great contrasts between the glamour of the latest express passenger locomotives and the continuing workaday duties of a host of ill-assorted pre-grouping classes. This is typified by this May 1939 photo showing former London & North Western Railway 5ft 6in 2-4-2 tank locomotive No. 6704, from a batch built between 1890 and 1897, piloting the then relatively new Stanier Class 4P 2-6-4 tank locomotive No. 2600 with an Oxford-bound train at Bletchley.
RMA9906

EDINBURGH The formation of the 'Big Four' railway companies sounded the death knell for the elegant three-cylinder Pacifics of the North Eastern Railway's Sir Vincent Raven that were introduced in 1922, and only five were ever built – the last three, surprisingly, in 1924. Despite their 6ft-diameter 200psi boilers, they proved no match for the A1 Pacifics of Nigel Gresley, who became the LNER's first Chief Mechanical Engineer. The last Raven Pacific to be built, No. 2404 *City of Ripon*, was fitted experimentally with an A1 boiler in 1929, but the results remained less than impressive, and all five locomotives had been withdrawn for scrapping by the end of 1937. In the accompanying photo the first to be built, No. 2400 *City of Newcastle*, is pictured at Edinburgh in 1931, and for the record, No. 2401 was named *City of Kingston upon Hull*, No. 2402 *City of York* and No. 2403 *City of Durham*. *RMA9920*

CREWE Seen in brand new condition at Crewe on June 28, 1935, the now-preserved Stanier 'Princess Royal' Pacific No. 6203 *Princess Margaret Rose* presents a picture of majesty and poise. *RMA10551*

DARLINGTON A cabside discussion appears to be going on as A3 Pacific No. 2575 *Galopin* awaits departure from Darlington Bank Top station in 1938. *RMA0849*

BEATTOCK Soon after its introduction in 1937 and glistening like new, streamlined 'Princess Coronation' Pacific No. 6220 *Coronation* is pictured at Beattock with the up 'Coronation Scot'. The other locomotives especially assigned to the task were Nos. 6221 *Queen Elizabeth*, 6222 *Queen Mary*, 6223 *Princess Alice* and 6224 *Princess Alexandra*. *RMA1272*

The Railway Magazine Archive Collection – The 1930s

15

Above: **WEST WYCOMBE** Throughout the 1930s the Great Western Railway's Chief Mechanical Engineer was Charles B. Collett, whose first batch of four-cylinder 'Castle' 4-6-0s, introduced in 1923, were virtually enlarged versions of Churchward's highly-acclaimed 'Stars'. So successful were the 'Castles' that some of the final 7000-series were built under British Railways. Heading the 'Cheltenham Flyer' during the 1930s, No. 5006 *Tregenna Castle* averaged a start-to-stop 81.68mph for the 77.25 miles from Swindon to London Paddington to take a new world record for steam traction. Here 'Castle' No. 5035 *Coity Castle* heads the heavy 4.05pm Paddington to Birkenhead train near West Wycombe on November 28, 1939. *RMA8294*

UNKNOWN LOCATION Looking like something from outer space when introduced in 1929, Gresley's sensational 'Hush-Hush' four-cylinder compound locomotive No. 10000 featured a marine-style water-tube boiler working at 450psi with two 12 x 26in high-pressure inside cylinders and two 20 x 26in low-pressure outside cylinders. It first ran in December 1929 and was fitted with a corridor tender for working prestige trains such as the 'Flying Scotsman'. Because of its experimental nature, it spent much more time inside Darlington Works that in service, and was finally rebuilt at Doncaster as a conventional three-cylinder W1 4-6-4 with A4-style streamlined cladding in 1936. The 'Hush-Hush' was pictured heading the 'Flying Scotsman' in the early 1930s. *RMA3897*

KINGS CROSS In its elegantly-rebuilt form, No. 10000 was pictured at King's Cross Shed in 1938. *RMA10000s*

CREWE Southport-bound train as former London & North Western Railway four-cylinder 'Claughton' 4-6-0 No. 5927 *Sir Francis Dent* pilots parallel-boiler 'Royal Scot' 4-6-0 No. 6124 *Lion* at Crewe in the early 1930s. *RMA1270*

The Railway Magazine Archive Collection – The 1930s 17

HULLAVINGTON A striking example of a Great Western 'Castle' 4-6-0 at speed as No. 5002 *Ludlow Castle* reaches Hullavington with a Paddington to South Wales express circa 1939. RMA0482

STIRLING This evocative picture of Scottish motive power at Stirling in 1938 is dominated by former Caledonian Railway Pickersgill 60 Class 4-6-0 No. 14652, but taking water to the left is former Highland Railway Drummond 'Castle' Class 4-6-0 No. 14686 *Urquhart Castle*. *RMA0379*

CHAPEL-EN-LE-FRITH Judging from the choking smoke trail, the fireman must have been shovelling on the coal as Stanier 'Jubilee' 4-6-0 No. 5627 *Sierra Leone* was pictured near Chapel-en-le-Frith with a Manchester to London express in the late 1930s. *RMA0351*

UNKNOWN LOCATION Putting down a tremendous tractive effort of 43,426lb, Gresley's mighty three-cylinder P2 2-8-2s were built specifically for handling heavy express trains over the difficult Edinburgh to Aberdeen route and were built between 1934 and 1936. The first of these, No. 2001 *Cock o'the North*, was pictured with a typically long train of teak coaches in the late 1930s. *RMA0797*

Right: **UNKNOWN LOCATION** Among the railways absorbed into the LNER was the North British Railway, and on July 20, 1931 NBR Holmes Class N (LNER Class D25) 4-4-0 No. 9595 was pictured at an undisclosed location. *RMA0542*

Below: **PERTH** Among the hugely diverse range of locomotives that found themselves in the hands of the London Midland & Scottish Railway in 1923 were the former Highland Railway 'Castle' Class 4-6-0s. *Duncraig Castle*, renumbered 14884, is seen at Perth in 1932. *RMA0922*

Below: **WALTON** Throughout the 1930s 4-4-0s remained the popular choice for lighter passenger duties. In Southern Railway days, former London & South Western Railway Drummond D15 No. 471 was pictured working a London to Salisbury train near Walton in 1938. *RMA 6562*

Above: **SHEFFIELD VICTORIA** Introduced in 1928, Nigel Gresley's three-cylinder D49/2 'Hunt' 4-4-0s, featuring Lentz rotary-cam poppet valves, were a development of the original 1927 D49/1 piston-valve locomotives, and 6ft 8in driving wheels gave both classes a fair turn of speed. The D49/2s were all named after famous hunts, with the top of each nameplate featuring a flying fox. No. 359 *The Fitzwilliam* backs on to a train at Sheffield Victoria on June 21, 1939. *RMA0785*

Above: **BUSHEY TROUGHS** A lineside photographer risks a soaking as original parallel-boiler Fowler 'Royal Scot' 4-4-0 No. 6111 *Royal Fusilier*, heading a London-bound express meat train, takes water at Bushey Troughs in 1935. *RMA1873*

Left: **LIVERPOOL LIME STREET** The LMS went through three Chief Mechanical Engineers – George Hughes, Sir Henry Fowler and E. J. H. Lemon – before William Stanier finally arrived from the Great Western Railway in 1932 and wasted no time in getting the urgent standardisation of that huge and sprawling railway's locomotive-building programme under way. Arguably his two-cylinder 'Black Five' 4-6-0s, introduced in 1934, were among the most successful mixed-traffic locomotives of all time, and one of them, No. 5101, was pictured beneath the canopy of Liverpool's Lime Street station in June 1935. *RMA2717 OV*

CONWAY CASTLE Fowler 'Royal Scot' 4-6-0 No. 6117 *Welsh Guardsman* makes an imposing sight at Conway Castle with the Euston-bound 'Irish Mail' on August 8, 1939. Note the Great Western and North Eastern vans on the right.
RMA0215

Above: **WATERLOO** The boiler size of four-cylinder Southern Railway Maunsell 'Lord Nelson' 4-6-0 No. 852 *Sir Walter Raleigh* is accentuated as it gets away from London Waterloo with an 11.30am Sunday express to Bournemouth circa 1932. *RMA1984*

Above right: **YORK** The powerful mixed-traffic Hughes/Fowler 'Crab' 2-6-0s played an important role throughout the LMS period, and one of these, No.2767, is seen on a passenger working at York in July 1937. *RMA10673*

Right: **DAWLISH** Only nine of Churchward's 4700-class 2-8-0s, introduced in 1919, were ever built by the Great Western Railway, and although they became known as 'Night Owls' because most of their fast freight workings took place at night-time, their useful 5ft 8in driving wheel diameter meant that they were often pressed into service on long and heavy main line passenger trains as well. No. 4707 was pictured on such a duty at Dawlish during the 1930s. *RMA6889*

Above: **GLASGOW CENTRAL** Built in maroon and gold streamlined form, LMS 'Princess Coronation' Pacific No. 6225 *Duchess of Gloucester* was virtually new when pictured at Glasgow Central Station in 1938. *RMA1502*

Right: **SHAP** Built in the handsome conventional form that William Stanier always preferred, LMS Pacific No. 6232 *Duchess of Montrose* climbs Shap with the down 'Mid-Day Scot' around 1939. *RMA9442*

HULLAVINGTON Despite the glamour of some of the express trains of the 1930s, goods traffic remained the top earner for all 'Big Four' railway companies. The former Great Central Railway Robinson 2-8-0s were built in large quantities for the Army's Railway Operating Division for service both during and after the First World War, but many were sold on to various pre-Grouping railway companies when the conflict ended. Some made their way to the Great Western Railway, where they continued to be known as 'RODs' (and were compared, inevitably, with Churchward's impressive 2800 2-8-0s). Embellished with a Great Western-style chimney and safety-valve bonnet, 'ROD' No. 3035 was pictured on a down goods train near Hullavington on September 28, 1939, by which time Britain was at war with Germany again. *RMA2606*

The Railway Magazine Archive Collection – The 1930s

Above: **SPALDING** In ex-works condition and now classified as an LNER 04, Robinson 2-8-0 No. 6557 heads a coal train through Spalding, Lincolnshire, and heads towards March in this circa 1930 photo. *RMA7546*

Below: **YORK** On the LNER, the sleek mixed-traffic three-cylinder V2 2-6-2s, introduced in 1935, became one of Gresley's finest locomotive designs. One of the few to be named, No. 4806 *The Green Howard, Alexandra Princess of Wales's Own Yorkshire Regiment*, is seen in all its apple green glory after the naming ceremony. *RMA6368*

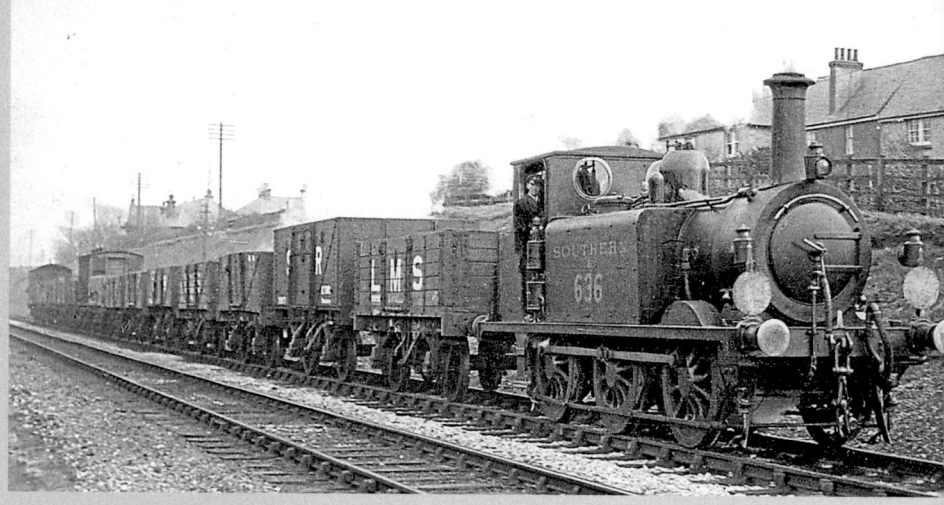

Above: **HADLEY WOOD** Prestige passenger trains were often in the hands of V2s, and on such duties they were well up with the best. Here No. 4817 bursts from the Greenwood Tunnel at Hadley Wood with a down 1930s 'Yorkshire Pullman'. *RMA0761*

Above right: **TWIXT SEAFORD AND NEWHAVEN** Because of their very low axle weight, the tiny Stroudley A1 and A1X 0-6-0 tank locomotives, built from 1873 onwards for working suburban services on the London Brighton & South Coast Railway, lasted well into 'Big Four' (and even British Railways) ownership. In Southern Railway days, A1 No. 636 paints a delightful portrait as it heads a Seaford to Newhaven local goods train circa 1930. *RMA8112*

Right: **KEYNSHAM** Among the Great Western Railway's best-loved passenger locomotives were the famous inside-cylinder, double-framed 'Bulldog' 4-4-0s built under William Dean from 1898 onwards. Built in January 1904 and withdrawn in March 1948, No. 3396 *Natal Colony* was pictured on a Westbury to Bristol train near Keynsham in 1935. *RMA1135*

The Railway Magazine Archive Collection – The 1930s

Above left: **SWINDON** Looking glorious after being newly-outshopped from Swindon Works in the 1930s, 'Bulldog' 4-4-0 No.3390 *Wolverhampton*, built in 1903, lost its nameplates when it was rebuilt as an 'Earl' with a 'Bulldog' chassis and 'Duke' boiler. Reflecting this mixture, the 'Earls' were to become more commonly known as 'Dukedogs'. *RMA6075*

Above: **BARMOUTH** A timeless setting as a Great Western Railway 'Bulldog' 4-4-0 crosses the Barmouth Viaduct with an eight-coach train in the 1930s. *RMA5883*

Left: **CODFORD** Great Western 'Bulldog' 4-4-0 No. 3364 *Frank Bibby* makes easy work of a lightweight Salisbury train near Codford in 1938. Built in February 1903, it was withdrawn under British Railways ownership in June 1949. *RMA2961*

Above: **SHAP** At the beginning of the 1930s, double-headers like this were commonplace on the heavy West Coast Main Line trains of the LMS. Former London & North Western Railway inside-cylinder 'Prince of Wales' 4-6-0 No. 5757 pilots former Lancashire & Yorkshire Railway Hughes four-cylinder 4-6-0 No. 10456 as they pass Shap summit with a Glasgow to Liverpool express. *RMA2979*

Above right: **TEBAY TROUGHS** Another very early 1930s double-header, this time comprising three-cylinder LMS Midland Compound No. 1124 a former Lancashire & Yorkshire four-cylinder Hughes 4-6-0, is seen on Tebay water troughs with an up express from Aberdeen. *RMA2767*

Right: **HOLMWOOD** With regulators well open, former South Eastern & Chatham Wainwright 'Flying Bedstead' B1 4-4-0 No. 1443 (with its 7ft driving wheels) and former London, Brighton & South Coast Railway Marsh H2 Atlantic No. 2424 *Beachy Head* hustle a long passenger train at Holmwood circa 1937. *RMA6550*

The Railway Magazine Archive Collection – The 1930s

Right: **BERWICK** Former Great Eastern Railway Holmes inside-cylinder B12 4-6-0 No. 8501, complete with feed water apparatus by ACFI (Societe l'Auxiliaire des Chemins de Fer et de l'Industrie), was pictured at Berwick while en route to the LNER's Great North of Scotland section on November 30, 1930.
RMA2006

Top far right: **RAMSGATE** Another nostalgic shot from the 1930s as Marsh H2 Atlantic No. 2424 *Beachy Head*, sporting Southern Railway livery, is seen at Ramsgate shed. Note the old coaches in the background.

Right: **FOLKESTONE** It's eight beats to the bar as Southern Railway Maunsell 'Lord Nelson' 4-6-0 No. 861 *Lord Anson*, with its original small chimney, heads an up continental express at Folkestone Junction during the summer of 1934.
RMA1338

TWIXT TAUNTON AND EXETER The wind snatches away the exhaust as Great Western Railway 'Bulldog' 4-4-0 No. 3361, whose original *Edward VII* nameplates had been removed in 1927, works a Taunton to Exeter stopping train in 1939. *RMA1136*

WATERLOO Capable of handling loads of 450 tons, Maunsell's V Class three-cylinder 'Schools' 4-4-0s of the Southern Railway were designed specifically for the tightly-restricted Hastings line, but ended up on many other duties, including fast trains to Portsmouth for which their 6ft 7in driving wheels made them ideal. In light green and with a self-trimming tender, No. 932 *Blundells* was pictured at Waterloo station with the 12.30pm to Bournemouth on May 27, 1939. *RMA2151*

Above: **UNKNOWN LOCATION** One of the more successful experimental locomotives of the 1930s was Stanier's famous steam-turbine 'Turbomotive' No 6202, the third of the 'Princess Royal' Pacifics that were introduced in 1933. Built in 1935, it featured a long forward turbine on the left-hand side, and a much shorter reversing turbine (as seen here) on the other. It spent much of its time working heavy trains between London Euston and Liverpool Lime Street, but remained unnamed until it was rebuilt as a conventional four-cylinder Pacific in 1952 and finally named *Princess Anne*. Featuring a 'Duchess' front end, it remained a unique member of the class, but tragically, just a few months after rebuilding, it was written off in the Harrow & Wealdstone disaster of October that year. *RMA5661*

Right: **ARDLEIGH BANK** Former Great Eastern Railway inside-cylinder 4-6-0 (LNER B12) No. 8579 works hard up Ardleigh Bank, Essex, with a Yarmouth express in 1932. *RMA3896*

Left: **UNKNOWN LOCATION** Three-cylinder parallel-boiler Fowler 'Royal Scot' 4-6-0 No. 6127 *Novelty* is prepared for a 'Night Scot' duty in the early 1930s. Before the arrival William Stanier's big Pacifics, and the consequent rebuilding of the 'Royal Scots' with taper boilers, these original 'Scots' were the premier express locomotives on the West Coast Main Line. Many bore old LNWR names such as *Novelty* (one of the locomotives that entered the Liverpool & Manchester Rainhill Trials in 1830), but No. 6127 was eventually renamed *The Old Contemptibles*. The name *Novelty* finally ended up on Stanier 'Jubilee' 4-6-0 No. 5733, one of the last of the class to be built. *RMA8418*

Above: **UNKNOWN LOCATION** Before the introduction of the Stanier 'Black Five' 4-6-0s in 1934 (of which no fewer than 842 were built between then and 1951), the Hughes/Fowler 'Crab' 2-6-0s, with their large inclined outside cylinders, were among the most important mixed-traffic locomotives on the LMS. One of these, No. 13000 was pictured in works grey in 1932. *RMA4167*

Left: **COLWYN BAY** For many years, 'Black Five' 4-6-0s were the prime movers on timetabled trains and holiday excursions from Liverpool and Manchester to the North Wales Coast. On August 8, 1939, No. 5232 was pictured near Colwyn Bay with a Chester to Llandudno train. *RMA3865*

Left: **AVIEMORE** The Hughes/Fowler 'Crab' 2-6-0s ranged far and wide over the LMS system, and here No. 13105 passes beneath a magnificent signal gantry at Aviemore on August 11, 1933. *RMA7286*

KING'S CROSS The unique LNER W1 4-8-4, rebuilt as a conventional three-cylinder locomotive from the experimental water-tube boiler 'Hush-Hush' No. 10000, graces the turntable at King's Cross in 1938. *RMA9182*

Right: **CREWE WORKS** In the boiler shop at Crewe, the side bar is set for the boiler frame of a 'Jubilee' 4-6-0 on February 7, 1935. *RMA8777*

Below: **BARMOUTH** With some members of the class seeing overseas service in both world wars, the Great Western 'Dean Goods' 0-6-0s, built at Swindon under the regime of William Dean between 1883 and 1899, gained something of a 'war horse' reputation. At its peak, the class numbered 260, and No. 2572 was pictured at Barmouth station in June 1939. Despite their name, members of the class were often seen on passenger duties throughout their long lifetimes. *RMA6091*

UNKNOWN LOCATION Perhaps the most unsightly express steam locomotive design to operate on Britain's railways was that of Dugald Drummond's 10 four-cylinder T14 4-6-0s built at Eastleigh Works for the London & South Western Railway in 1911 and 1912. The bulbous splashers over the 6ft 7in driving wheels and wide cylinder covers quickly earned them the nickname 'Paddlebox'. The cylinders were set in line, with derived motion from the outside Walschaerts valve gear working the inside cylinders, but the class proved underpowered, heavy on coal and prone to axlebox overheating, and was rebuilt by the Southern Railway's Richard Maunsell with partial success in the early 1930s. The T14s soldiered on into the Second World War, but all had gone by 1951. In its original form, No. 447 steams through a wide cutting strewn with wildflowers. *RMA11742*

ELGIN The elegant D40 4-4-0s came into the LNER from the Great North of Scotland Railway. The class was split between the 13 Neilson, Reid & Co-built class Vs of 1899 and the eight superheated F class versions of 1920, six of them built by the North British Locomotive Company and the remaining two by the GNSR's Inverurie Works. They remained a familiar sight for many years until finally withdrawn from service between 1947 and 1958. Only the superheated former Class F versions were named, and one of these, No. 49 *Gordon Highlander*, is preserved. No. 6848 *Andrew Bain* was pictured in typically clean condition at Elgin in the 1930s.
RMA0599

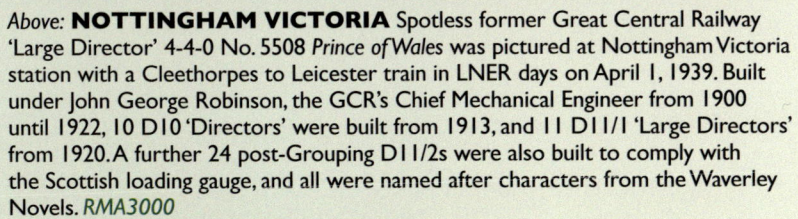

Above: **NOTTINGHAM VICTORIA** Spotless former Great Central Railway 'Large Director' 4-4-0 No. 5508 *Prince of Wales* was pictured at Nottingham Victoria station with a Cleethorpes to Leicester train in LNER days on April 1, 1939. Built under John George Robinson, the GCR's Chief Mechanical Engineer from 1900 until 1922, 10 D10 'Directors' were built from 1913, and 11 D11/1 'Large Directors' from 1920. A further 24 post-Grouping D11/2s were also built to comply with the Scottish loading gauge, and all were named after characters from the Waverley Novels. *RMA3000*

Above right: **MARKINCH** There's a lovely clean exhaust as LNER D11/2 4-4-0 No. 6382 *Colonel Gardiner* heads an Edinburgh to Dundee slow passenger train near Markinch in the summer of 1933 *RMA0559*.

Right: **BEATTOCK** LMS three-cylinder 'Baby Scot' 4-6-0 No. 5538, named *Giggleswick* in 1938, takes no prisoners as it assaults Beattock Bank near Greskine Box with a 1930s Liverpool-Edinburgh express. *RMA2886*

Above left: **BALLINLUIG JUNCTION** Shadows from a lattice girder footbridge are cast onto the smokebox door of former Highland Railway 'Small Ben' 0-6-0 *Ben-y-Gloe*, carrying its LMS number 14397, as it waits at Ballinluig Junction with a local goods train in the late 1930s. The last survivor of the class, No. 54398 *Ben Alder*, was stored for many years from 1953 in the hope that it would be preserved, but despite all efforts to save it, the little locomotive was cut up in 1967. *RMA3341*

Above: **LETCHWORTH** Burnished to perfection, LNER 'Super Claud' D16 4-4-0 No. 8783 leaves Letchworth Garden City with an ordinary-looking passenger train circa 1933. There must have been a reason for the locomotive's outstanding condition, but this is not known. After the 1923 Grouping, several sub-classes were developed from Holden's legendary Great Eastern Railway 'Claud Hamiltons' of the early 1900s. *RMA9255*

Left: **TWIXT LIVERPOOL STREET AND SOUTHEND** In workaday condition, D16 'Claud Hamilton' 4-4-0 No. 8848 works a Liverpool Street to Southend train in August 1933. *RMA2997*

The Railway Magazine Archive Collection – The 1930s

41

Right: **KENTISH TOWN** The location is Kentish Town in the 1930s, and the locomotive is former Midland Railway Johnson 3F 0-6-0T No. 7200, from a batch dating from 1899, fitted with condensing apparatus. *RMA2758*

Left: **CRAIGENTINNY** An LNER D11/2 4-4-0 in all its glory as No. 6397 *The Lady of the Lake* stands at Craigentinny in this 1930s photo. *RMA1919*

FORT WILLIAM The LNER K2 2-6-0s were a prominent feature of the West Highland Line for many years, and No. 4693 *Loch Sheil*, still with its basic original cab, was pictured at Fort William MPD in August 1933. In view of the blizzard conditions that were often encountered on the line, some of the class were subsequently fitted with much-needed side window cabs. *RMA1956*

CARLISLE The 22 Reid Atlantics, introduced in three batches from 1906 until 1921, were the heaviest and most powerful of their type to operate on the North British Railway, and in superheated form and with a boiler pressure of 200psi, their work on both the Waverley route and the main line between Edinburgh and Aberdeen was truly outstanding. Their appeal was enhanced by the superb Scottish names they carried, and they continued the good work under LNER ownership until the withdrawals began from 1933 onwards. In LNER apple green express passenger livery at Carlisle in the 1930s, No. 9905 *Buccleuch* makes an imposing sight, but sadly not a single example of the class was preserved. *RMA0547*

Above: **GOWHOLE SIDINGS** Former Midland Railway LMS 3F 0-6-0 No. 3307, from a class built from 1885 onwards, heads a down goods train near Gowhole Sidings, New Mills, Derbyshire, in the 1930s. *RMA5114*

Above right: **SHEFFIELD MIDLAND** LMS 2P 4-4-0 No. 324 waits with a Chesterfield train at Sheffield Midland station on June 21, 1939. *RMA1378*

Right: **ANDSELL** Former Lancashire & Yorkshire Railway Aspinall 0-6-0 No. 12208 heads a Blackpool excursion train near Andsell in the 1930s. *RMA1878*

Left: **WILLBRAHAM ROAD** Although dating back to the 1890s, the former Great Central Railway 0-6 0s that were classified J10 by the LNER worked tirelessly in shunting yards, on pick-up goods trains and local passenger services until well into British Railways days. In this picture from the 1930s, No. 5131 heads a local passenger train at Willbraham Road station, in Whalley Range, Manchester, on the former Fallowfield loop line from Manchester Central via Chorlton-cum-Hardy and Guide Bridge. The station closed in July 1958. *RMA0851*

Below: **SHAP FELL** Former Lancashire & Yorkshire Railway four-cylinder Hughes 4-6-0 No. 10466 toils over Shap Fell with a long northbound goods train. The steam in the distance is from the banker, a former Caledonian Railway 3F 0-6-0. *RMA5724*

READING A picture in power and majesty as four-cylinder 'King' 4-6-0 No. 6022 *King Edward II* makes light work of a Torbay-bound train at Reading circa 1936. Introduced in 1927 under the supervision of the Great Western Railway's Chief Mechanical Engineer Charles B. Collett (1922-1941) the 'Kings', with their 6ft 6in driving wheels and high tractive effort of 40,300 lb, could haul the longest and heaviest trains on the railway, but at a cost of very restricted route availability on account of their weight. *RMA3243*

The Railway Magazine Archive Collection – The 1930s   47

ADDISON ROAD STATION LMS G2A 0-8-0 No. 9037 passes through Addison Road station with a typical goods train of the era circa 1939. Note the platform lighting and the general tidiness of the scene. *RMA6241*

Left: **WELLS ROAD** Great Western Railway Dean Goods 0-6-0 No. 2412 was pictured near Wells Road with a Frome to Bristol train on October 31, 1939. *RMA4316*

Above: **RETFORD** Introduced in 1924, the short, squat three-cylinder K3 2-6-0s were another of Gresley's outstanding LNER mixed traffic designs, and quickly gained a reputation for being able to handle anything that could be thrown at them. In this classic 1930s shot, No. 2766 heads southwards with an express train at Retford North Signal Box. *RMA0847*

Left: **NOTTINGHAM VICTORIA** The handsome lines of former Great Central Railway Class 1 (LNER B2) inside-cylinder 4-6-0 No. 5433 *Sir Sam Fay* are seen to advantage as it waits at Nottingham Victoria station in the 1930s. Only six of the powerful mixed-traffic locomotives were built at Gorton Works between December 1912 and December 1913, and all were withdrawn between 1944 and 1947. The others were named *City of Lincoln*, *City of Manchester*, *City of Chester*, *City of London* and *City of Liverpool*. *RMA0653*

Left: **SAM FAY** Born in Hampshire in 1856, Sir Sam Fay joined the London & South Western Railway as a clerk at the age of 16 and went on to become the last General Manager of the Great Central Railway.

Below: **LICKEY INCLINE** LMS 4F 0-6-0 No. 4528 works hard with a goods train on the Lickey Incline, backed by two 3F 'Jinty' 0-6-0 tank engines, in 1939. *RMA3332*

Below: **TWEEDMOUTH JUNCTION** The Raven three-cylinder B16 4-6-0s were introduced in 1920 to a North Eastern Railway design, and clusters of them remained in places like Leeds, York and Darlington until the early 1960s. They proved worthwhile locomotives on goods and passenger services alike, and No. 911 was pictured at Tweedmouth Junction in 1933. *RMA0825*

Above: **SOUTHPORT** Former Great Central Railway D9 4-4-0 No. 6020 pilots former North Eastern Railway B16 4-6-0 No. 936 with an excursion train at Southport circa 1934. *RMA8898*

SPALDING Former Great Central Railway J10 0-6-0 No. 5817 passes Spalding, Lincolnshire, with an up coal train in this 1930s picture. *RMA5799*

READING A nice Great Western Railway pairing as 'Dean Goods' 0-6-0 No. 2579 and 6100 class Prairie tank No. 6163 are seen together at Reading MPD in the 1930s. *RMA3160*

Right: **DARLINGTON** This undated picture of ex-works LNER Raven Pacific No. 2402 *City of York* was taken outside Darlington Works. *RMA2925*

Below: **LUNE GORGE** LMS parallel-boiler 'Royal Scot' 4-6-0 No. 6135 *Samson* (later named *The East Lancashire Regiment*) makes smoky progress through the Lune Gorge on July 4, 1935. *RMA2986*

BROMLEY SOUTH On July 30, 1932, former South Eastern & Chatham Railway Wainwright D class 4-4-0 No. 1742 leaves Bromley South with a long Chatham line excursion train made up of SE&CR six-wheel stock. *RMA13915*

UNKNOWN LOCATION Introduced in 1935, William Stanier's 8F 2-8-0s were modern freight locomotives whose numbers were boosted considerably by the outbreak of the Second World War. No. 8033, one of a batch of 69 ordered by the LMS and built by the Vulcan Foundry at Newton-le-Willows, Lancashire, in 1936-7, was brand new when this picture was taken in 1936. In 1943 the cheaper-to-build Ministry of Supply 'Austerity' 2-8-0s, together with a small batch of 2-10-0s, made further 8F orders from the War Department unnecessary. The 8Fs continued to be built until 1946. *RMA7834*

MANCHESTER CENTRAL Another C13 4-4-2T, No. 5055, was pictured at Manchester Central on July 29, 1939. *RMA5763*

MICKLE TRAFFORD LNER C13 class 4-4-2T No. 5115, formerly of the Great Central Railway's 9K class, heads a Cheshire Lines Committee train near Mickle Trafford in the 1930s. Introduced in 1903, some of these useful Robinson-designed locomotives were fitted with push-and-pull equipment, and all passed into BR ownership in 1948, with the last one not being scrapped until 1960. *RMA8227*

REDHILL Another really atmospheric scene from times gone by as Southern Railway U1 class 2-6-0 No. 1898 waits with an up train at Redhill station in the 1930s. RMA2467

SAUNDERTON Introduced in 1903, Churchward's legendary 2800 class 2-8-0s were thoroughly modern-looking and efficient two-cylinder freight locomotives that enjoyed long and productive lives. No. 2871 was pictured at Saunderton with a long Acton to Bordesley Junction goods train circa 1938. *RMA2393*

NOTTINGHAM VICTORIA Footplatemen bestowed the nickname 'Black Pigs' upon Robinson's powerful 9Q mixed-traffic 4-6-0s (LNER B7s) because of the four-cylinder locomotives' insatiable appetite for coal. Introduced in 1921, shortly before the Grouping, the 9Qs were actually a very capable design that proved equally at home on fast freights, excursion trains and even express passenger turns, and batches were built at Gorton Works, the Vulcan Foundry and Beyer, Peacock & Co. Even after the Grouping, the LNER ordered a final batch of 10 from Gorton. In this 1930s photo, No. 5033 shows off its long lines at Nottingham Victoria station. *RMA5964*

DUMPTON PARK Southern Railway U1 2-6-0 No. 1902 was in charge of a northbound 'Sunny South Special' near Dumpton Park in the 1930s. *RMA 2116*

Left: **BLAIR ATHOLL** Seen at Blair Atholl 83 years ago in November 1936 is former Highland Railway 'Ben' 4-4-0 No. 14397. *RMA8344*

Below: **SOUTHPORT LORD STREET** Former North Eastern Railway three-cylinder B16 4-6-0 No. 936 was pictured at Lord Street, Southport, on March 23, 1934. *RMA9967*

UNKNOWN LOCATION The LMS 'Jinty' 0-6-0 tank engines weren't just for shunting, as No. 16582 adequately proves as it heads a North London 'bogie train' in the 1930s. *RMA2745*

TWEEDMOUTH Large and small-boilered locomotives from both the North Eastern and North British Railways cluster together in the roundhouse at Tweedmouth in the 1930s. *RMA0827*

BARKSTON LNER A4 Pacific *Mallard* and its seven-coach train, including the former North Eastern Railway's 1906-built dynamometer car immediately behind the locomotive, were pictured at Barkston, on the East Coast Main Line, immediately before the record-breaking 126mph run on Sunday July 3, 1938.

Above: **UNKNOWN LOCATION** These were the ordinary working men who made it all possible. Both driver Joe Duddington and inspector Sid Jenkins firmly believed that 130mph could have been attained were it not for a couple of track restrictions that had to be observed on the day. The rpm of the 6ft 8in driving wheels at 126mph was calculated at almost 530, equating to more than eight times per second.

Index of locations

A
Addison Road Station 47
Andsell 44
Ardleigh bank 33
Aviemore 35

B
Ballinluig Junction 40
Barkston 63
Barmouth 29, 36
Beattock 14, 39
Berwick 31
Blair Atholl 60
Bletchley 11
Bromley South 54
Bushey troughs 21

C
Carlisle 43
Chapel-en-le-Frith 19
Codford 29
Colwyn Bay 34
Conway Castle 22
Craigentinny 41
Crewe 9, 13, 16
    works 36

D
Darlington 13, 53
Dawlish 23
Doncaster 10
Dumpton Park 59

E
East Coast Main Line 10
Edinburgh 12
Elgin 38
Euston 6

F
Folkstone 31
Fort William 42

G
Glasgow Central 24
Gowhole Sidings 44
Gretna 7

H
Hadley Wood 28
Harringay 2
Holmwood 30
Hullavington 17, 26

K
Kentish Town 41
Kettering 9
Keynsham 28
King's Cross 15, 35

L
Letchworth 40
Lickey Incline 49
Liverpool Street 21
Lune Gorge 53

M
Manchester Central 56
Markinch 39
Mickle Trafford 56

N
Nottingham Victoria 39, 48, 58

P
Perth 20

R
Ramsgate 31
Reading 46, 52
Redhill 57
Retford 48

S
Sam Fay 49
Saunderton 58
Shap 24, 30
Shap Fell 45
Sheffield Midland 44
    Victoria 21
Southport 50
    Lord Street 60
Spalding 27, 51
Stirling 18
Swindon 29

T
Tebay Troughs 30
Tweedmouth 62
    Junction 50
Twixt Liverpool Street and
    Southend 40
Twixt Seaford and Newhaven 28
Twixt Taunton and Exeter 32

U
Unknown location 2, 15, 19, 20, 33, 34, 37, 55, 61, 63

W
Walton 20
Waterloo 23, 32
Wells Road 48
West Wycombe 15
Willbraham Road 45
Wood Green 2

Y
York 5, 23, 27

The **RAILWAY** *Magazine* *Archive Collection*